A UNIVERSE OF TERMS

Religion and the Human

Winnifred Fallers Sullivan and Lisa Sideris, editors

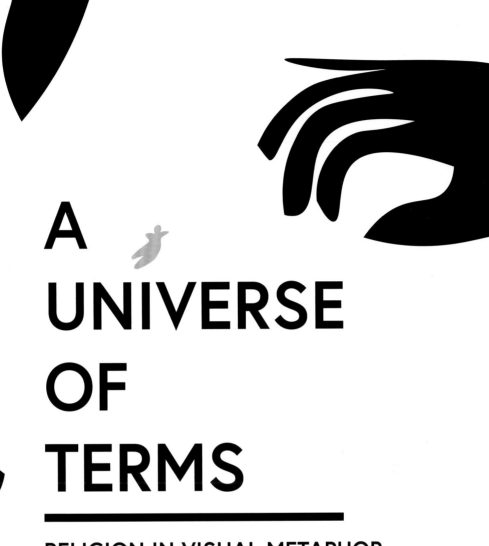

A UNIVERSE OF TERMS

RELIGION IN VISUAL METAPHOR

MONA ORABY
and EMILIE FLAMME

INDIANA UNIVERSITY PRESS

This book is a publication of

Indiana University Press
Office of Scholarly Publishing
Herman B Wells Library 350
1320 East 10th Street
Bloomington, Indiana 47405 USA

iupress.org

Manufactured in China

First Printing 2022

Cataloging information is available from the Library of Congress.
ISBN 978-0-253-06410-3 (hdbk.)
ISBN 978-0-253-06417-2 (pbk.)
ISBN 978-0-253-06411-0 (web PDF)

CONCEPT, NARRATIVE, and DESIGN
Mona Oraby and Emilie Flamme

PREFACE
Mona Oraby

BOOK LAYOUT and ILLUSTRATIONS
Emilie Flamme

CONTENTS

Preface   xi–xxii

Acknowledgments   xxv–xxvi

Note on Quotations   xxix–xxx

Table of Terms   1

SPIRIT   3

ECONOMY   19

HUMAN   35

MEDIA   49

PERFORMANCE   67

SPACE/PLACE   85

MODERNITY   99

ENCHANTMENT/DISENCHANTMENT   117

Index   135

Bibliography   149

Preface

My eyes land on three shelves where I've stacked exhibition catalogs and artists' books horizontally because of their awkward size. One of these is *A Promise to Communicate* by Wangechi Mutu, known for her mixed-media collages on Afrofuturism and Black feminism.[1] At about 4 by 6 inches, the book is small enough to fit in your palm. It's based on Mutu's installation, "A Promise to Communicate," commissioned and exhibited in 2018 by the Institute of Contemporary Art (ICA) Boston. Consistent with her signature style, the reuse of found objects, Mutu reconfigured a map of the world using humanitarian aid blankets, sticks, stones, and pencils. But the world did not appear to me as the world—at first. From a distance the land masses looked like eraser shavings swept into gigantic mounds; their borders were clearly defined, yet the spaces between them slight.

This was the first exhibition that patrons saw—that I saw—as we entered the museum. As I neared, I recognized Africa as an island, rotated clockwise 90 degrees; Australia, flipped and also rotated, sat nestled between Côte d'Ivoire and Angola; Alaska, cut from Canada, floated between Russia and South America, each also estranged from their usual neighbors and suspended at odd angles. Amid our confusion, we were invited by Mutu to write on the wall, a request we accepted with some trepidation, recalling a common childhood scold. We penned messages to people we would never meet, who would read what we wrote and cover our marks with more graphite, not knowing whether north was North, south was South, east was East, or west was West. And where had all the oceans gone?

A Promise to Communicate captures in multiple mediums and at varying scales the relation an artist shares with those who engage her creative act.

This relation lives long past the moment of encounter. The book transfers onto translucent paper layers of text and symbols left by thousands of visitors. Bound together, these layers create a flip-book. Communicative acts within the museum thus form a permanent, yet portable, record of the exhibit. Without these inscriptions, "A Promise to Communicate" could not have fulfilled its purpose: for visitors to exchange in a shared space their unfettered ideas about what collectivity means and requires of us. The book also includes photographs of the installation at both its premiere and its closing; the former captures a wall bare but for Mutu's enormous collage, and the latter evinces a wall thick with graphite and visual codes. Added to the translucent paper and photographs is a conversation between Mutu and the exhibition curator.

Mutu, in her exhibition and her book, does not simply invert the familiar.[2] Instead, by playing with a form's relation to its parts and our relation to them, she compels new thought, language, and knowledge about ostensibly settled questions. To communicate, in Mutu's sense, is to transform and transgress, continuously, what we know or accept to be true.

*　*　*

Emilie Flamme was a student when we first met at Amherst College, where I held my first professorship. Emilie was not *my* student. We were never in a seminar together, I've never given her a grade, and I was not her departmental, college, or thesis adviser. Notably, the knowledge hierarchy typical of professor-student interactions did not structure ours. Looking back now, I see it was our conversations that solidified our bond. "Good conversation," says Vivian Gornick, "is dependent on a simple but mysterious fit of mind and spirit that cannot be achieved, it just occurs. It's not a matter of mutual interests or class concerns or commonly held ideals, it's a matter of temperament."[3] Emilie's gears and mine fit like adjacent pieces in a Clemens Habicht puzzle, not at the hard, outer edges but closer to the center or lower third, the differences between the pieces so subtle their alignment is a small victory.[4] We started thinking together on campus and through our .edu addresses. We soon became collaborators. Now we are coauthors.

Emilie first sought me out in her junior year while working on a final project, an illustrated text of post–civil war Lebanon, for a course taught by another professor. At the time, I was teaching a course called "Sectarian Modernity," which considers sectarianism and modernity as coemergent phenomena that structure thought and life transnationally. It owes its architecture to sociologists, historians, political scientists, and anthropologists who study Arab-West entanglement.[5] These scholars query knots variously called "sect," "sectarian," and "sectarianism"—and, by implication, "modern," "modernity," and "modernization." The course begins with life in those places—Lebanon, Iraq, and Syria—where sect-based differences are said to inhibit modern social affinities. I use graphic novels and memoirs by regional and diasporic Arab authors to teach students how and why these knots matter to our world.

When Emilie came to office hours we talked about our personal and professional connections to the Middle East. With five languages between us and an obsessive likeness in the way we talked about design, we nerded out on how to represent concepts visually. Soon after, Emilie needed to finish the assignment that had brought her to my office in the first place. I lent her some graphic memoirs and novels I assign for class: Riad Sattouf's series *The Arab of the Future*, Brigitte Findakly and Lewis Trondheim's *Poppies of Iraq*, Lamia Ziadé's *Bye Bye Babylon*, and several works by Zeina Abirached. Numerous conversations around these books fueled our collaborative thinking.

The events of spring and summer 2020 prompted a commitment, a necessity, to give our conversation a form. Everywhere, deep-seated thought patterns failed to explain or remedy the precarities of our moment, a realization made worse by a cutting fact: much of the massive and recurring loss of life (understood in the broadest sense) was preventable. Despite early warnings from epidemiologists, the novel coronavirus devasted communities worldwide, throwing into relief those most vulnerable to contagion. In the United States, communities of color, the working poor, and first-responders were hit particularly hard by the Covid-19 pandemic. The Movement for Black Lives, here and abroad, brought attention to two truths: the fact that Black life is vulnerable not only to excessive force but also to systemic failures in public health; the fact that as Americans reckoned with historic and ongoing legacies of racial oppression, over four million acres of California forest burned. Record-breaking lightning strikes and lapses in human judgment led to ecological disaster.

When colleges and universities pivoted online, old questions about accessibility in higher education became new again. Emilie and I talked a lot those days about the purpose of scholarship. We asked ourselves: How do we resist a racist, imperial, and extractive modernity when our lexicon is both indebted to and constrained by that same modernity? *A Universe of Terms: Religion in Visual Metaphor* is our answer to this question. The academic study of religion offers us a way to imagine collective life differently. Although religious studies as a field has only begun to confront the possibility of human extinction, scholars of religion write insightfully about the human as both catalyst of crisis and principal agent for its mitigation. Many scholars who are moving this conversation forward contributed to a multimedia project, "A Universe of Terms," hosted by *The Immanent Frame* (*TIF*), a digital publication of the Social Science Research Council. I was editor of that project and Emilie its content designer. *A Universe of Terms* illustrates a select number of terms and responses to those terms from that project, as well as some essays previously published on *TIF*. No new writing was solicited for this publication. Furthermore, we did not retain all the terms and contributions to the digital project. Those we included lend themselves to illustration within the original iconography developed by Emilie.

The outcome of our thinking, mine and Emilie's, is a graphic nonfiction book that acknowledges the significance of certain terms to the social sciences and the humanities, narrates their limitations, and shows why we need a structure for thinking them otherwise. It further urges the iterative rethinking of any new terms this exercise yields. I use "terms" here in four ways: to name time periods, as in the years 1945–1955; term limits, as in the length of time one may hold an office; concepts, like "modernity," "economy," and "human;" and forms of scholarly engagement—such as articles, edited volumes, and monographs—including the networks that yield these outputs. All four uses of the word "terms" attribute to their objects an outmodedness, whether present or eventual. Following from these meanings, we propose an alternative form for scholarly communication, one that calls some conventions into question (e.g., associations of seniority or pedigree with superior knowledge) while retaining others (e.g., engagement through citation) in order to initiate a conversation about new thought circuits and who they might include. We recruited the words of nearly two dozen distinguished scholars to heed a call bell hooks named in 1994: "[K]now beyond the boundaries of what is acceptable, so that we can think and rethink, so that we can create new visions."[6]

*   *   *

We were inspired initially by Nancy Levene. Levene is among the fifty-four invited contributors to "A Universe of Terms." When Emilie and I considered what our book would look like, it was Levene's example that gave us direction, although her response to the term "modernity," some might say, lacks such a thing: it is comprised entirely of quotations. Each quotation is a paragraph. There is no topic or concluding sentence, no sign posting, no thesis or summative statement. A reader's inclination to read (and write) from left to right and from top to bottom might orient her to the response. But Levene's adherence to conventional academic writing mostly stops there. Only this guidance is offered: "Note: The final word in each quote links to the quote's source; quotes internal to a quote link to the citation; in case of two final links, the first is to the original source, the second to the book in which it appears." Levene cites her sources and her source's sources, but does not tell us what we are supposed to understand from their content or their arrangement. Neither does she explain what those scholars may have overlooked nor justify her agreement with them. She sketches out a conversation, but does not name her contribution to it. Levene instead leaves us hanging.

What genre of writing is this? Expository, descriptive, persuasive, narrative? What is the thing Levene created? A treatise, an essay, maybe a curatorial statement? Scholars often corral a string of quotations into a Word document to map out a loose direction for our work. We press and prod our Play-Doh thoughts until they're firm enough to build Lego fortresses. Here, though, Levene provides no roadmap to help the reader navigate an ambiguous terrain. She offers up nothing to fill the space between the quotations. Had Levene published a draft? No. Emilie and I agreed: the brilliance of Levene's work is her selection and assembly of thinkers and their words, the invitation to the reader to make her own connections and to draw her own conclusions. We began to think differently. Maybe confronting our need for direction is the point. Maybe we've overlooked other ways of doing scholarship by obsessing over authorial intention. Maybe we've been asking the wrong questions. We began to ask different ones, like: Which conventions did Levene break to achieve the effect of her writing?

We intuit from Levene's example that traits attributed to good academic writing might well be arranged in different patterns—if the goal is to shake up and reorganize existing thought. For all the rule-breaking her example evinces, it is not without form. It has a shape. "A basic structural design underlies every kind of writing," explain William Strunk and E. B. White in *The Elements of Style*. "The first principle of composition, therefore, is to foresee or determine the shape of what is to come and pursue that shape."[7] When we confront our unmet expectations in Levene's response, we are jarred into thinking about what is not there. Levene "leave[s] the space of representation open," following Trinh Minh-ha; the space between her paragraphs, between the quotations, is not so much empty as it anticipates and holds space for the reader. Levene accepts the brief to write on modernity by "speaking nearby" rather than about, "which requires that you deliberately suspend meaning, preventing it from merely closing and hence leaving a gap in the formation process. This allows the other person to come in and fill that space as they wish."[8] By short-circuiting our well-worn thought and language patterns, Levene helps us to see how new connections are forged.

Besides the novel form of Levene's contribution, we were struck by its content—the arrangement of quotations that implicate us in a question, idea, or event. Take just one example: "The question to ask is not whether we can return the native to her authentic origin, but what our fascination with the native means in terms of the irreversibility of modernity." *Who* is asking that question? *What* is our fascination? Is this fascination continuous no matter *who* "we" are? Levene pulls this quotation from a chapter by Rey Chow, titled "Where Have All the Natives Gone?" Yet another question. And so, each quotation that Levene invokes also names a set of nested claims, objects, and queries. These constitute a constellation of references and conversations that reverse the knowledge arrow, pointing it from the scholar to the reader, who may or may not also be a scholar by training. All of these claims, objects, and queries tell a story about modernity and the relationships between self and other that obtain within it. *We* tell, narrate, and interpret story. "Where else can we go," asks George Saunders, "but the pages of a story, to prefer so strongly, react without rationalization, love or hate so freely, be so radically ourselves?"[9]

Levene and other contributors to the digital project entangled us in their clever use of language and form. I attribute this effect to one of two techniques: they either raised questions (as did Courtney Bender, Mark Cauchi, Birgit Meyer, and Winnifred Fallers Sullivan) or used the second person or the first-person plural (see the responses by Anthea Butler, Constance Furey, Paul Christopher Johnson, Susan Lepselter, Kathryn Lofton, Emily Ogden, John Durham Peters, Nathan Schneider, and Jonathan Sheehan). Sometimes a single author used both techniques (see the responses by Abou Farman, Christine Helmer, Webb Keane, Amira Mittermaier, William Robert, and Josef Sorett). Almost always, their personal story—indeed, their *persona*—could not be disassociated from what they wrote. Another set of scholars provide additional narrative glue for *A Universe of Terms*. By walking us through their research—whether shadow maps (Judith Weisenfeld), a musical call and response (Vaughn Booker), a clinician's office (Omnia El Shakry), or Shakespeare's theater (Paul Yachnin)—they stretched our imaginations. We learned and became invested in their claims.

As close readers of the digital project, Emilie and I were also interested in using form, style, shape, color, and line to advance an argument whose basis we found in the scholars' claims. This meant thinking with and beyond the written word. We decided to create a graphic text, a kind of hybrid visual-literary object, to evince how scholarship is translated, transposed, and transformed. And so, *A Universe of Terms* is part graphic novel, part art book, and part nonfiction text. The word is its character. We created new illustrations for *A Universe of Terms* that are consistent with the modernist style of the digital project and expand its visual lexicon. Where the featured text is rich in concrete nouns and active verbs, the illustrations are derived directly from those words or their referents. When she viewed the draft manuscript, Birgit Meyer called this practice "citation through images," a description we find quite apt. If the original text does not name an immediate visual object, Emilie and I propose one. Here, the word speaks in visual metaphor. *A Universe of Terms*—the selection, arrangement, fragmentation, and visualization of text within it—is entirely a work of interpretation by Emilie and me. Every spread is the outcome of a conversation about language and image. Every spread refuses the false binary often imposed on this pairing.

If Levene's model spurred Emilie and me to think unconventionally, it was our mutual love for visual culture paired with expressive language that we turned to for form, by which I mean we returned to the objects that anchored our original encounter: graphic novels and memoirs. In his essay "Enduring Love of the Second Person," Mohsin Hamid explains how comic books and sci-fi and the dramatic monologue of Albert Camus's *The Fall* made him realize "that 'you' could simultaneously be audience and character and maker." The second person address compels one to consider "how feelings already present inside a reader—fear, anger, suspicion, loyalty—could color a narrative so that the reader, as much as or even more than the writer, is deciding what is really going on."[10] Emilie and I nested scholarly claims in a visual language to achieve the effect that Hamid describes. *A Universe of Terms* invites scholars to think again and anew about visuality's integration with thought. We flatten the knowledge hierarchies that attribute authority to knowers of a particular kind, suggesting instead that what readers, whomever they are, see, infer, and emote enables scholarship to thrive.

At a manuscript workshop we hosted, Webb Keane called *A Universe of Terms* an "archipelago of feeling." Our provocation to the reader to feel as she reads, the scholar to anticipate feeling as she writes, is no doubt inspired by the scholars we feature here. We intuited from their words the possibility of transformative change, just as a protracted period of foment and exhaustion called out for new thinking on a huge scale. These scholars touched a nerve, namely the literal and figural museums of our childhoods, spaces we associate with creative potential. The objects housed in these spaces are somewhat specific to where Emilie and I grew up, to exhibitions we've seen in person or in catalogs, but this specificity exceeds geographic terms. Familiarity, typically rooted in the concept of home, is for us less a place than a memory collection of things we observed, carried, ate, and discarded. Proximate in age (Emilie is a Gen-Zer, I'm a millennial), we both claim a cosmopolitan upbringing. For us, international flights are as synonymous with adolescence as Cabbage Patch dolls, games of checkers, and Magic 8 Balls.

*   *   *

In an interview about his monograph, *Blind Spot*, Teju Cole explains the complementarity of various media, how his writing for the public and making images "is of a piece." "I used to think they were really separate," he says. "Now I realize that looking at the world, making images, writing about images, writing about things that are not images, all of it is an attempt to testify to having been here and seen certain things, having looked at the world with a kind eye but an eye that is not ignoring questions of justice and history."[11] *A Universe of Terms* accepts that the desire to witness coexists with the interminable fallibility of human vision, fallible not only during certain moments—like when an optometrist dilates our pupils or when we enter a dark room. Obstructed vision, we might say, is a kind of universal and permanent condition. It makes us human, and we share its effects. Striving also makes us human. What we do together matters to our collective life, as scholars or students, yes, but more as thinking beings responsible for a world bigger than ourselves.

Working within scholarly conventions to show the yet unexplored possibilities for their flexibility was a joyful experience amid the sorrow of 2020. We found within scholarship a way to revise and replenish our language and our thought, which gave us hope. Emilie and I credit a broad scholarly community, we say *our thinking relies and builds on yours*. It was important for us to publish this book with a university press, that we walk through the peer review process, so that it be seen by scholars as an academic work. Our project also tugs at the boundaries of academic publishing. *A Universe of Terms* combines the complementary skills of two women, differently situated in our education, and yet of one mind that we could be cocreators— that we could think and collaborate and produce a work of scholarship. The editors of this book series, the faculty board at Indiana University Press, and its director thought similarly. Our sense of cocreative possibility could not have been realized if it was ours alone.

Research and teaching are tools for our collective renovation and improvement. They also anticipate creative acts yet unknown. *A Universe of Terms* stages conversations between thinkers who likely would not all find themselves in the same room. That is to say, this book imagines what a transdisciplinary reception of scholarly associations would look like if other creatives—illustrators, directors, designers—were also invited. What brought Emilie and I together to bring these scholars together—in word, image, line, color, and shape—were the questions: Is a more inclusive, responsible, and communicative future possible? How do we get there?

*   *   *

The table of terms outlines the cartography of the book. We designed a narrative that builds momentum from the start to its last illustrated page. Each chapter is also its own story. The chapters can be read or viewed in sequential order, or individually, to consider synergies between and among nonadjacent chapters. The index lists the names of the scholars we cite and the text that is cited in the order that it was originally written. We on occasion shortened the text using ellipses. Italics that appear in the book are original to how the text appears in the featured scholars' writing.

The essays from which we draw the quotations are available in full on the website of *The Immanent Frame*. Media we read and listened to as we developed the book are listed in the bibliography.

MONA ORABY

NOTES

1. Wangechi Mutu, *A Promise to Communicate* (Madrid: Ivorypress, 2019).

2. The "south-up" map, for instance, rotates a conventional world map at 180 degrees, rendering North down and South up. Similarly, the "inverse map" turns land into water, and water into land. In both cases the trick is not difficult to see. Mutu's installation, by contrast, displaces water, severs land masses, and rearranges continents such that at first sight none of its component parts appear to comprise a map at all.

3. Vivian Gornick, *Approaching Eye Level* (New York: Picador, 1996), 103.

4. Clemens Habicht is a designer, director, and illustrator. His *COLOUR* jig-saw puzzles, launched in 2014, range from 100 to 5000 pieces, and are among his best-known works—available in two- and three-dimensions. No matter the size, difficulty, or shape of the puzzle, the task is the same: "to place each colour exactly in relation to every other colour." Clemens Habicht, "Colour Puzzles," accessed May 21, 2021, https://www.clemenshab icht.com/design/colour-puzzles.

5. Among them Lara Deeb, Toby Dodge, Omnia El Shakry, Suad Joseph, Dina Rizk Khoury, Ussama Makdisi, Timothy Mitchell, Bassel Salloukh, Lisa Wedeen, Benjamin White, and Max Weiss.

6. bell hooks, *Teaching to Transgress: Education as the Practice of Freedom* (New York: Routledge, 1994), 12.

7. William Strunk, Jr. and E.B. White, illus. Maira Kalman, *The Elements of Style*, 4th ed. (New York: Penguin, 2007), 31.

8. Trinh T. Minh-ha, "'There is No Such Thing as Documentary': An Interview with Trinh T. Minh-ha," interview by Erika Balsom, *Frieze*, November 1, 2018, https://www.frieze.com/article/there-no-such-thing-documentary-interview-trinh-t-minh-ha.

9. George Saunders, *A Swim in the Pond in the Lake: In Which Four Russians Give a Master Class on Reading, Writing, and Life* (New York: Random House, 2021), 386.

10. Mohsin Hamid, *Discontent and its Civilizations: Dispatches from Lahore, New York, and London* (New York: Riverhead Books, 2015), 104.

11. Teju Cole, "Finding My Way into a New Form: An Interview with Teju Cole," interview by Steve Paulson, *The Millions*, July 5, 2017, https://themillions.com/2017/07/finding-way-new-form-interview-teju-cole.html.

Acknowledgments

This book would not have been possible without the Religion and the Public Sphere Program at the Social Science Research Council, which hosts *The Immanent Frame* (*TIF*), and the Henry Luce Foundation, which supports the program and Mona Oraby's editorship of *TIF*. Our thanks to Daniel Vaca and Olivia Whitener, who assisted in the solicitation and editing of the essays published in the multimedia project "A Universe of Terms," on which *A Universe of Terms* is based.

We are grateful to numerous scholars who, through their research and teaching, advance the academic study and public understanding of religion. We wish to thank in particular those who contributed to "A Universe of Terms," and further, whose writing for *TIF* is excerpted here and who participated in the workshops we hosted in summer 2020. Courtney Bender, Mark Cauchi, Abou Farman, Constance Furey, Omnia El Shakry, Christine Helmer, Webb Keane, Nancy Levene, Birgit Meyer, John Durham Peters, William Robert, Nathan Schneider, Josef Sorett, Winnifred Fallers Sullivan, Judith Weisenfeld, and Paul Yachnin asked important questions at a critical stage in the book's development.

Emily Ogden and Kathryn Lofton were unable to attend the workshops, but their influence appears throughout the book. We want to acknowledge the deep impressions they have made on our thinking. Unbeknownst to Emily, sentences in her essay on "spirit" plucked Pappachi's moth from *The God of Small Things* and nestled the metaphor-as-agent in our consciousness. We begin the book with her words, our nod to this happy coincidence. Katie, writing on "economy," set loose many of our closely guarded memories of taste and touch. We thank Katie for her constant reminder that the senses matter to thought. Her whole person exemplifies the kind of thinking this book propounds.

Many people affiliated with Indiana University supported the publication of *A Universe of Terms*, and have supported us as scholars and cocreators. We extend our thanks to Winni Sullivan and Lisa Sideris for including the book in the Religion and the Human series at Indiana University Press. We thank our editor, Gary Dunham, for believing in this project and for facilitating its review and production. The entire IU Press team—from editorial to marketing to publishing—took great care in answering our many questions. Constance Furey taught a chapter of *A Universe of Terms* in her "Original Sin" course at IU before the book went into production. Thank you to Constance and IU graduate student Hannah Garvey for making this opportunity possible and to the more than fifty undergraduates who offered candid assessments of the work.

Omnia El Shakry and Nancy Levene read the penultimate version of the preface with characteristic precision. They identified exactly those words or phrases that could be better worded and better phrased. Thank you, Omnia and Nancy, for your close reading. Nancy: You gave life to the form this book would eventually take.

One scholar whose words do not appear in the book will nevertheless have a lasting impact on how we view academic collaboration. Sally Promey not only reviewed the book for the press but has also lent her unwavering support to us and to this project ever since. Her encouragement, suggestions, and guidance prompted key adjustments to the manuscript. We are grateful to have been spurred by Sally to tell and illustrate a more intuitive story.

Note on Quotations

All text that appears in *A Universe of Terms* is a quotation. There are multiple layers of authorship in some sentences or phrases. A sentence or phrase that appears in the book without any quotation marks means the featured scholar (e.g., a scholar listed in the index) is the author of the text. A sentence or phrase with double quotation marks indicates one layer of authorship removed from the featured scholar. A sentence or phrase that appears with double and single quotation marks indicates two layers of authorship removed from the featured scholar. Below are examples of each of these uses:

Ex. 1, from the chapter on SPIRIT: Whatever *spirit* is—and the term has many meanings—you usually have to get rid of some other encumbering things in order to get at it.

This sentence is a direct quotation from Emily Ogden's essay, "spirit." She authored the entire sentence and so no quotations enclose this text in *A Universe of Terms*.

Ex. 2, from the chapter on SPIRIT: [T]he spirit of America is, as one historian put it, "the encounter of black and white."

This sentence is a direct quotation from Josef Sorett's essay, "spirit." He is the author of the sentence. At the same time, Sorett cites another scholar, David Wills. Wills's words appear in double quotation marks in the excerpt above and within *A Universe of Terms*.

Ex. 3, from the chapter on MODERNITY: "In what sense does modernity belong to a closed entity, a 'geo-body' named Europe?"

This sentence is a direct quotation from Nancy Levene's response, "modernity." Paul Gilroy is the author of the sentence, and Thongchai Winichakul is the source of a concept internal to it. In *A Universe of Terms*, we use double quotation marks to indicate Gilroy's authorship of the sentence and single quotation marks to indicate his reference to Winichakul.

A UNIVERSE OF TERMS

TABLE
OF
TERMS

SPIRIT [3]

ECONOMY [19]

HUMAN [35]

MEDIA [49]

PERFORMANCE [67]

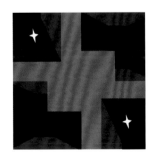

SPACE/PLACE [85]

MODERNITY [99]

ENCHANTMENT/
DISCHANTMENT [117]

SPI

RIT

Whatever *spirit* is—and the term has many meanings—you usually have to get rid of some other encumbering things in order to get at it.

The spirit of Spirit, if you will, is demolition.

is
theirs
to
Kick.

The moth skates through the damaged web. Demolition actually works this time.

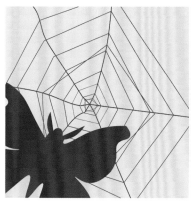

[S]pirit is never only gaseous or metaphysical. It always links up with *things*, like airline, writing, teen, face of the waters, pants. Then, too, spirit moves in verbs like incorporate, possess, descend, hover, fill, and have. And spirit settles near adjectives like holy, ancestral, or free. Verbs and adjectives materialize and spatialize an otherwise vaporous word. They turn spirit tangible, push it into text and flesh incarnate.

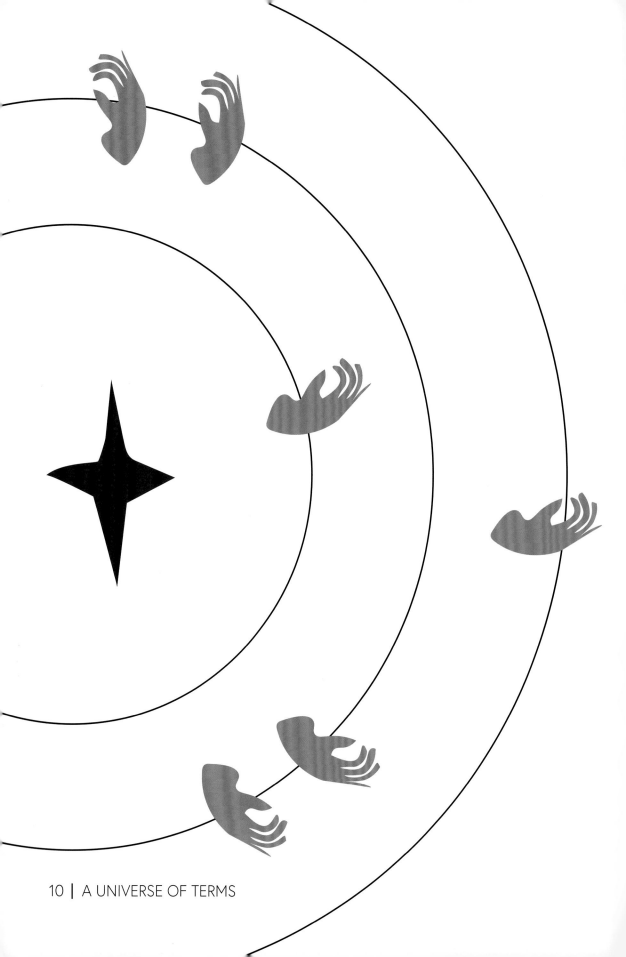

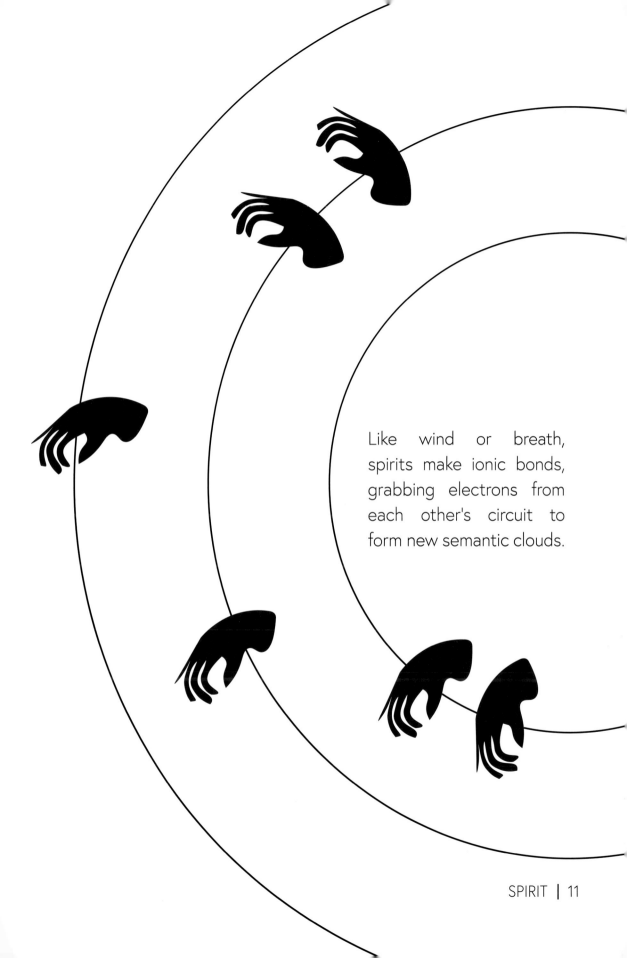

Like wind or breath, spirits make ionic bonds, grabbing electrons from each other's circuit to form new semantic clouds.

The Spiritual Exercises. The Spirit of 1776. Spirit of an age, *Zeitgeist*. We've got spirit! A spirited opposition. Spiritual awakening. Spiritual warfare. The Spirit of Christmas Past. *Esprit de corps*. Spirit possession. Spirit Airlines. Holy Spirit. Espírito Santo, Brazil. "Whoa, spirit / Watch the heavens open (yeah) / Spirit, can you hear it callin'?" sings Beyoncé. Karl Marx: We are infused by the spirit of the state. Émile Durkheim's spirit of society. Conception among the Arunta, wrote Sigmund Freud, is experienced as a reincarnated spirit entering the mother's body. Spiritism. Smells like teen spirit. Spirit-writing. Spirited away. Such a free spirit. . . . That's the spirit! Ancestor spirit. And the Spirit of God moved upon the face of the waters. "Shop Esprit for dresses, tops, pants, skirts, shoes and accessories."

Spirit gives a name to outside forces
that impinge on inner will. Even more,
it undoes the very idea of a discrete
split between inner and outer.

What happens when spirit(s) is tethered to an adjective? A racial modifier, for instance? Does making spirit black help to clarify things?

SPIRIT

[T]he spirit of religion in America is, as one historian put it,

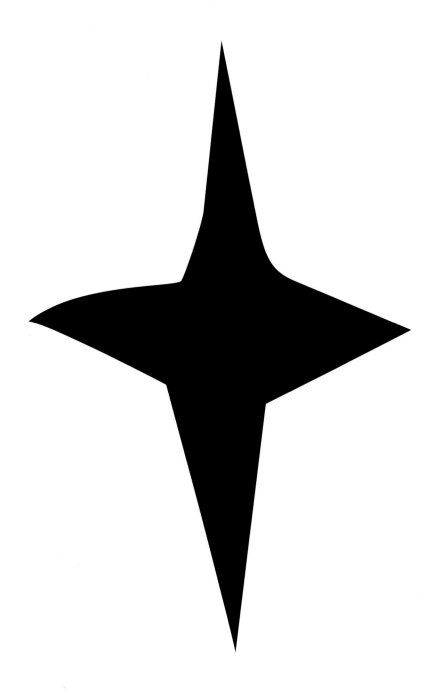

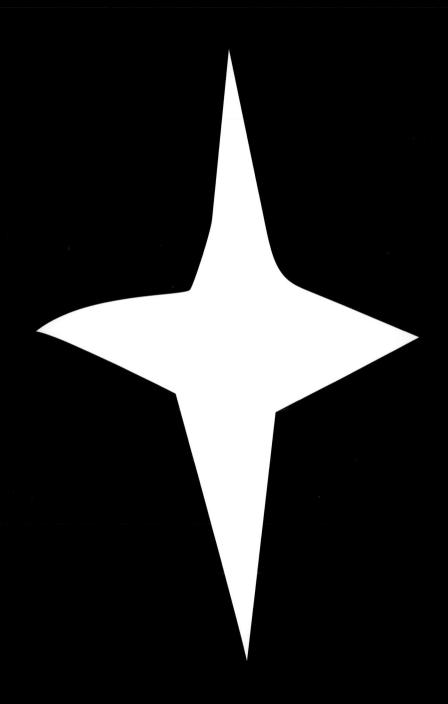

"the encounter of black and white."

Economy is not about money or things. Economy is the practice of constraint toward money and toward things. Economy is a synonym for denial, for constraint, for restraint.

███████████████████████████

Particular religions feel differently about payroll.

But every religion counsels on how not to be controlled by coin.

Writing about the commodity,

Marx used adjectives such as
queer,
metaphysical,
theological,
transcendent,
mystical,
fantastic, and
magical

(or, in the German original,
vertrackt,
metaphysisch,
theologisch,
mysteriös,
übersinnlich,
wunderlich,
mystisch,
rätselhaft,
geheimnisvoll).

GODS
SPIRIT
GODS
SPIRITS
SPIRITS GODS
GODS SPIRITS GODS SPIRIT
GODS SPIRITS GODS
SPIRITS GODS SPIRITS GODS SPIRITS
SPIRITS GODS
SPIRIT
GODS
SPIRITS
GODS
SPIRITS
GODS
SPIRITS

What might it mean to think of the economy with the gods and spirits fully present? How can we take seriously the queer, mystical, metaphysical, and theological underpinnings (and iterations) of the economy?

GODS SPIRITS GODS
GODS SPIRITS GODS SPIRITS
GODS SPIRITS GODS
SPIRITS GODS SPIRITS GODS SPIRITS
GODS SPIRITS GODS
GODS SPIRIT
GODS
SPIRITS
GOD

SPIRITS GODS SPIRITS GODS SPIRITS GODS SPI
GODS SPIRITS GODS SPIRITS GODS SPIRITS GO
SPIRITS GODS SPIRITS GODS SPIRITS GODS SPI
GODS SPIRITS GODS SPIRITS GODS SPIRITS GO
SPIRITS GODS SPIRITS GODS SPIRITS GODS SPI
GODS SPIRITS GODS SPIRITS GODS SPIRITS GO
SPIRITS GODS SPIRITS GODS SPIRITS GODS SPI
GODS SPIRITS GODS SPIRITS GODS SPIRITS GO
SPIRITS GODS SPIRITS GODS SPIRITS GODS SP
GODS SPIRITS GODS SPIRITS GODS SPIRITS GO
SPIRITS GODS SPIRITS GODS SPIRITS GODS SP
GODS SPIRITS GODS SPIRITS GODS SPIRITS GO
SPIRITS GODS SPIRITS GODS SPIRITS GODS SP
GODS SPIRITS GODS SPIRITS GODS SPIRITS GO
SPIRITS GODS SPIRITS GODS SPIRITS GODS SP
GODS SPIRITS GODS SPIRITS GODS SPIRITS G
SPIRITS GODS SPIRITS GODS SPIRITS GODS SP
GODS SPIRITS GODS SPIRITS GODS SPIRITS G
SPIRITS GODS SPIRITS GODS SPIRITS GODS SP
GODS SPIRITS GODS SPIRITS GODS SPIRITS G
SPIRITS GODS SPIRITS GODS SPIRITS GODS SF
GODS SPIRITS GODS SPIRITS GODS SPIRITS G
SPIRITS GODS SPIRITS GODS SPIRITS GODS SF

GODS SPIRITS GODS SPIRITS GODS SPIRITS GO
SPIRITS GODS SPIRITS GODS SPIRITS GODS SPI
GODS SPIRITS GODS SPIRITS GODS SPIRITS GO
SPIRITS GODS SPIRITS GODS SPIRITS GODS SPI
GODS SPIRITS GODS SPIRITS GODS SPIRITS GO
SPIRITS GODS SPIRITS GODS SPIRITS GODS SPI
GODS SPIRITS GODS SPIRITS GODS SPIRITS GO
SPIRITS GODS SPIRITS GODS SPIRITS GODS SPI
GODS SPIRITS GODS SPIRITS GODS SPIRITS GO
SPIRITS GODS SPIRITS GODS SPIRITS GODS SPI
GODS SPIRITS GODS SPIRITS GODS SPIRITS GO
SPIRITS GODS SPIRITS GODS SPIRITS GODS SPI
GODS SPIRITS GODS SPIRITS GODS SPIRITS GO
SPIRITS GODS SPIRITS GODS SPIRITS GODS SPI
GODS SPIRITS GODS SPIRITS GODS SPIRITS GO
SPIRITS GODS SPIRITS GODS ECONOMY GODS
GODS SPIRITS GODS SPIRITS GODS SPIRITS GO
SPIRITS GODS SPIRITS GODS SPIRITS GODS SPI
GODS SPIRITS GODS SPIRITS GODS SPIRITS GO
SPIRITS GODS SPIRITS GODS SPIRITS GODS SPI
GODS SPIRITS GODS SPIRITS GODS SPIRITS GO
SPIRITS GODS SPIRITS GODS SPIRITS GODS SPI
GODS SPIRITS GODS SPIRITS GODS SPIRITS GO

Not secularizing the economy means leaving space for the gods and spirits whenever and wherever they turn up.

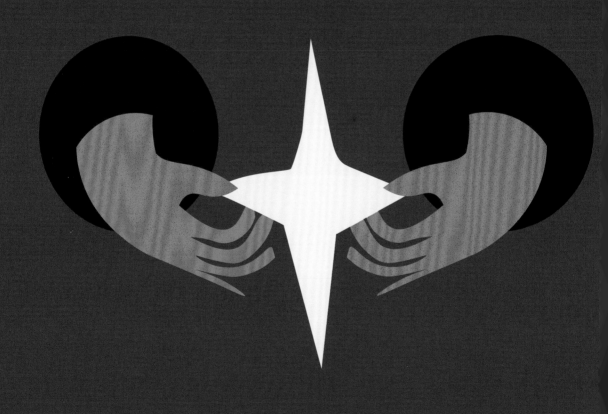

Here,

divine action

(and not a fetishized "economy")

decenters human labor.

The scriptural assertion that "the poor you will always have with you" leads back from the God's eye perspective to the second person of address, "you," and its partner, the first person plural, "us."

And these pronouns bring us back to the street, where the most visible of the poor challenge the passerby to ask: Do you count as one of us?

━━━━━━━━━━━━━━━━━━━

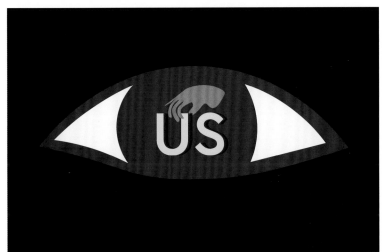

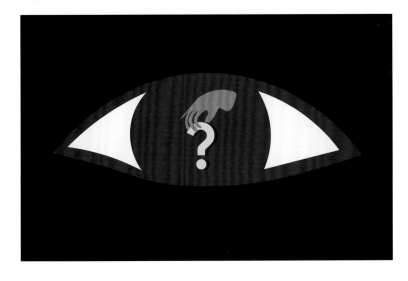

HUN

1AN

Human living—resistance in the face of the inevitable, and orientation to love in the face of annihilation. Theologians look to those places of resilience. They wonder at glimpses of dignity amid the decrepitude.

Human living is a daily struggle to make ends meet; a blank stare into an unlit tunnel; the horror at what is unspeakable yet real.

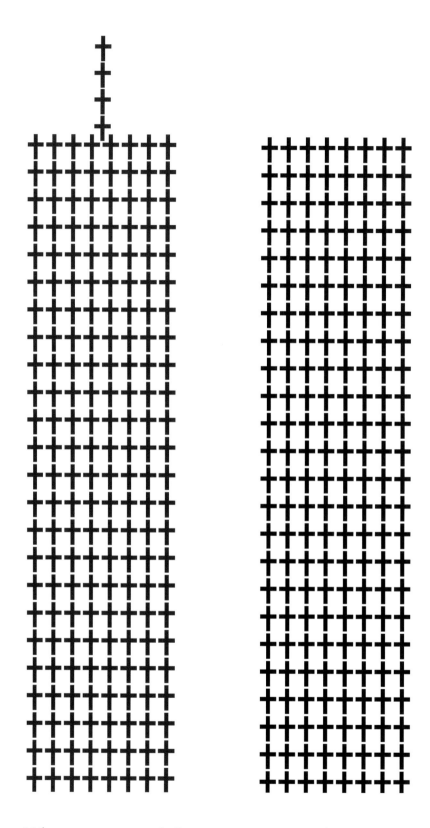

What are crosses? Can crosses—can *the* cross—
be a sign of the human?

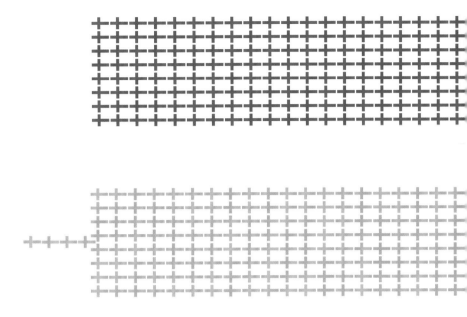

The cross came to be understood as preceding and prefiguring the Christ. In other words, those who study the cross see a deeply ambiguous and shifting symbol, one not easily reduced to either religious or secular.

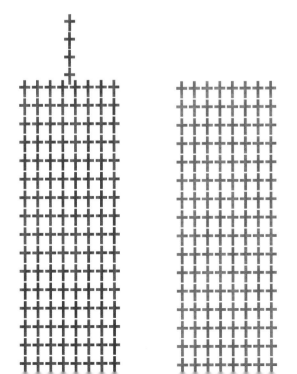

THE

WHO

In her essential article about how humanity came to be a racist category, Sylvia Wynter identifies Luther's era as a turning point. When Renaissance humanists "degodded" man, Wynter argues, the human became a biocentric category. Absent God, she observes, "Race becomes the answer that the secularizing West would now give to the Heideggerian question as to the who, and the what we are."

THE

W
H
A
T

I do not think, as Wynter implies, that having a god keeps humans in check, but instead that putting a god or gods in the mix might help us to think the human better.

GODS ARE WE

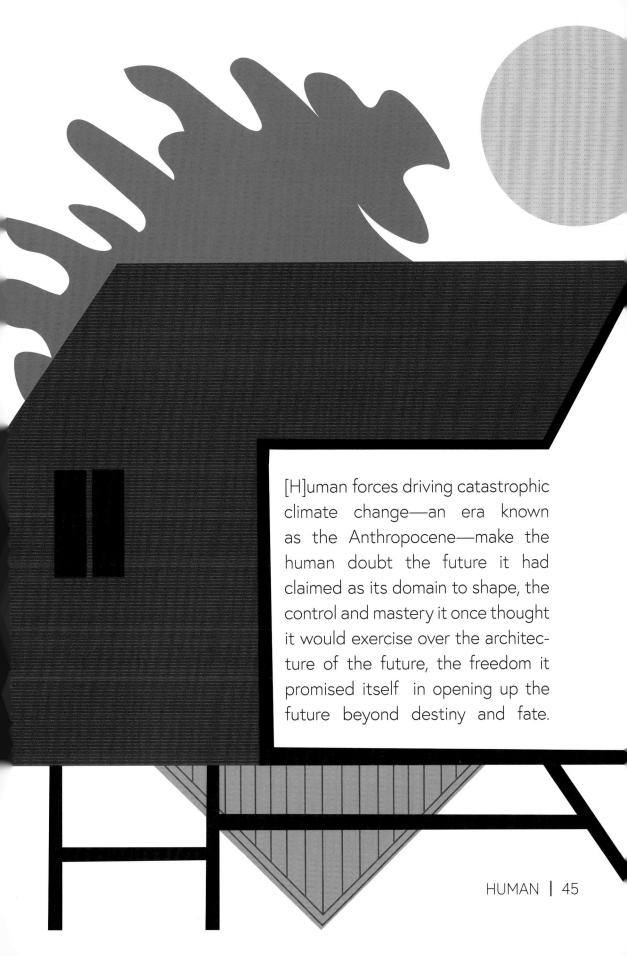

[H]uman forces driving catastrophic climate change—an era known as the Anthropocene—make the human doubt the future it had claimed as its domain to shape, the control and mastery it once thought it would exercise over the architecture of the future, the freedom it promised itself in opening up the future beyond destiny and fate.

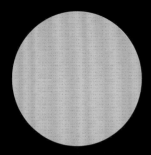

[T]here is no universal human world
that is going to end; rather, under the
rhetoric of universal humanity, people
are mobilizing, again, to save particular
worlds from destruction.

Which human world do you want to see end?

ME

DIA

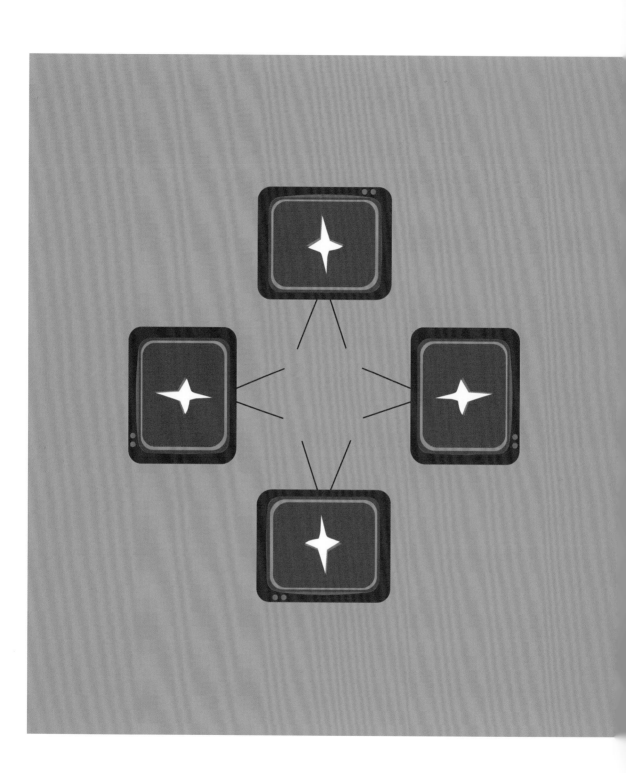

Media vary historically.

Media turn on borders and interfaces.

Media have grammars.

Media combine nature and culture.

Media have ontological effects.

In 1963, my parents, with three kids (aged five, three, and one) in tow and one more on the way . . . got a small black-and-white television set. . . . TV signals would bounce off of buildings, creating small lags in transmission and *Doppelgänger* on screen, but often the signals would never even arrive, leaving us with no more picture than an apocalyptic scene of warring ants jousting at high-speed.

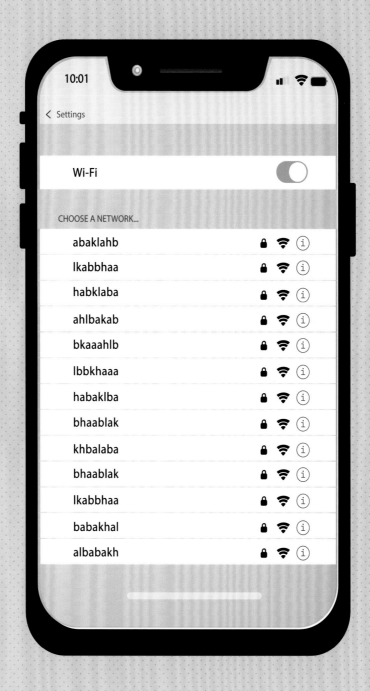

Nothing's quite as spooky as logging into Wi-Fi in a hotel or apartment building and seeing all those anonymously intimate networks pop up, a broadcast Kabbalah of secret names and private jokes you will never be privy to.

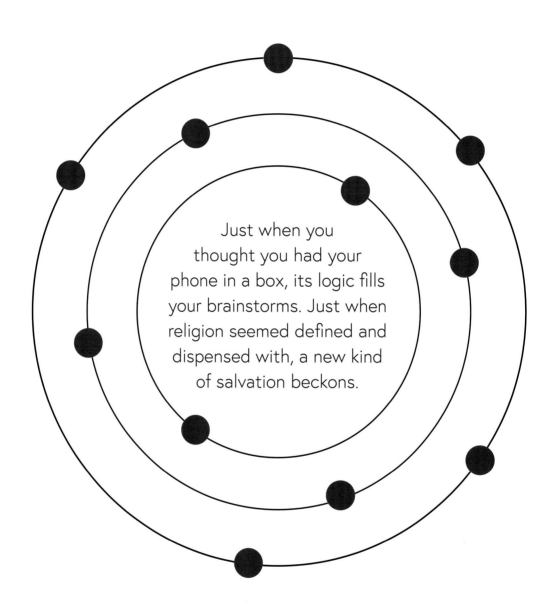

Just when you
thought you had your
phone in a box, its logic fills
your brainstorms. Just when
religion seemed defined and
dispensed with, a new kind
of salvation beckons.

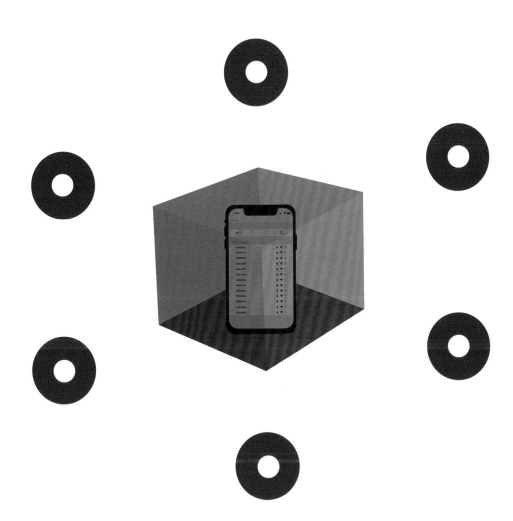

What might happen when we put the discarded *legbawo* of the Ewe, and similar images of other African peoples, in conversation with the discarded images of Mary and Jesus (as done by way of experiment in the Bode Museum Berlin)?

What might these objects, that became "matter out of place" in their present, secular contexts, tell us

about human striving for power and powers in our deeply entangled, postcolonial world?

—МОНГРАДАН—

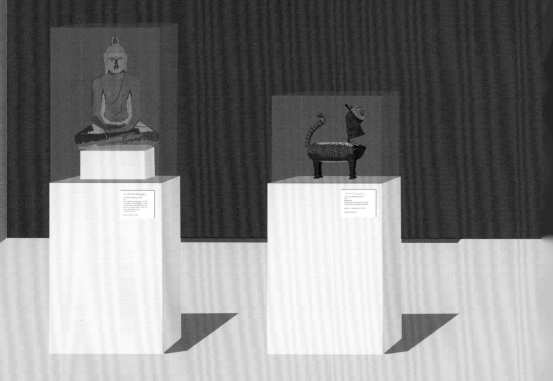

How do such old religious media matter in secular contexts? Which memories, stories, and powers can they mediate and transmit?

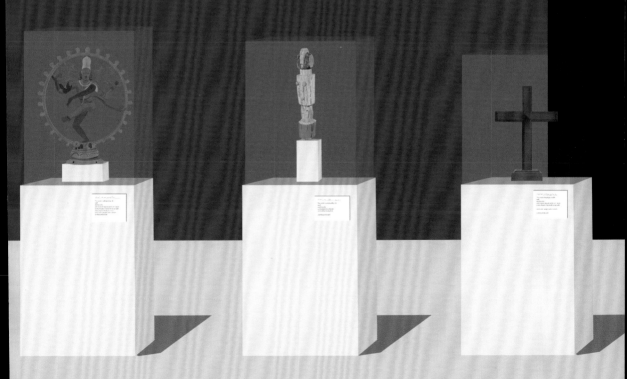

PERFOR

MANCE

A performance is some kind of action that changes something in the real world.

"Performance" also means play-acting, doing or saying something that changes nothing in the real world.

[W]e could say that Shakespeare's theatrical faith workshop became a space for "communicative action."

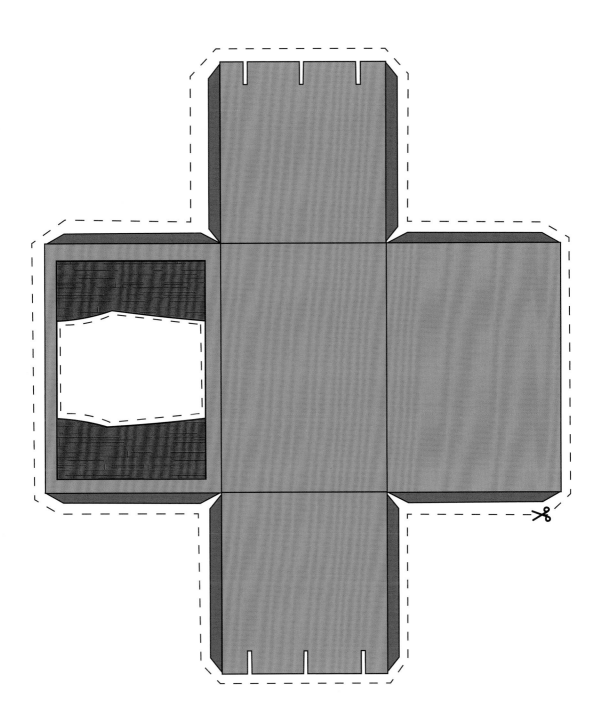

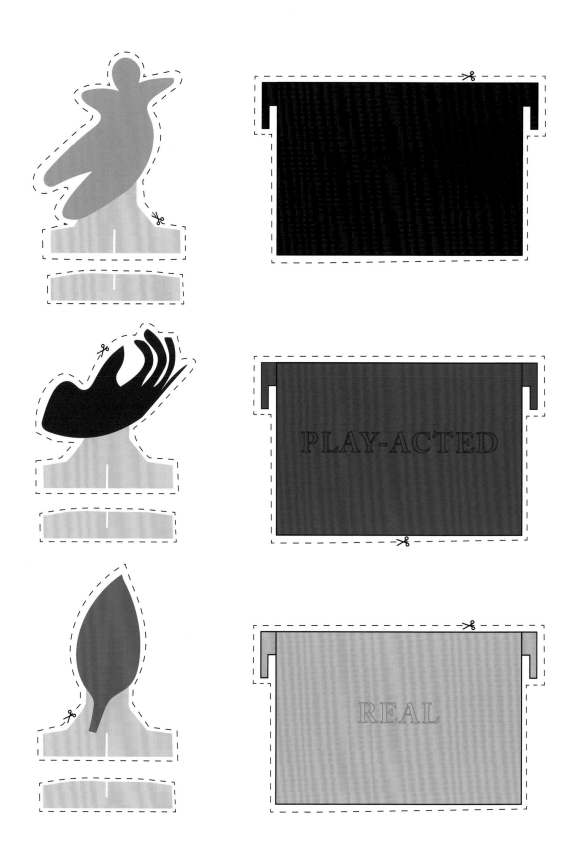

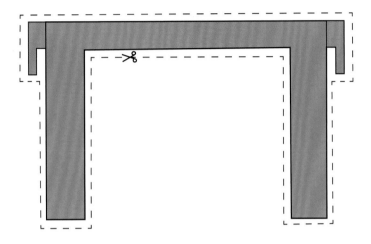

Shakespeare's faith workshop . . . invited the playgoers to give expression to their religious feeling and thinking by way of their responses to the action unfolding on stage, to recognize the different faith-based emotions and thoughts of other playgoers, and to begin to grasp how faith itself is performed—both accomplished as a real thing in the world and play-acted as an invention of the mind.

RE

A musical call and response between brass and reeds opens the 1933 compositionfor Cab Calloway and His Orchestra, "Harlem Camp Meeting." A voice asks, "What's this comin' off here?" and after a brief pause, reflects, "It's more like one of them good ol' revival days here. A camp meeting! Yowza, yowza!" Next comes a clarinet solo, and the inquiring voice assumes the role of a narrator in remarking, "There's a dear brother got happy on that clarinet, look at him. Greeeat day!" As the clarinet solo continues, the narrator interjects affirmative responses: "Tell me all about it, brother. Tell me all about it, now." The narrator then refers to the "brother" as "son" and tells him to "Get ready for this scat sermon I'm gonna give you here." The narrator produces a wordless vocal melody, accompanied by syncopated chimes replicating the sound of distant Sunday church bells.

On Holy Saturday 1294, an Umbrian woman found herself in a sepulcher with Christ's dead body. The woman kissed Christ's breast, then Christ's mouth. She placed her cheek on Christ's cheek. Then Christ placed his hand on her other cheek. Christ pressed the woman's body close to his in an embrace. Christ whispered lovingly to the woman, though Christ's eyes and lips remained closed.

The woman was Angela of Foligno (c. 1248–1309), a widow, a lay Franciscan, a mystic. Angela's sepulcher scene came in the twenty-fourth step of her twenty-six-step spiritual itinerary. Her itinerary included other extraordinary scenes. Angela denuded herself before a crucifix. She saw eyes appear in eucharistic bread-bodies. She bathed lepers, then drank the bathing water. She drank blood from, and later entered, Christ's side wound.

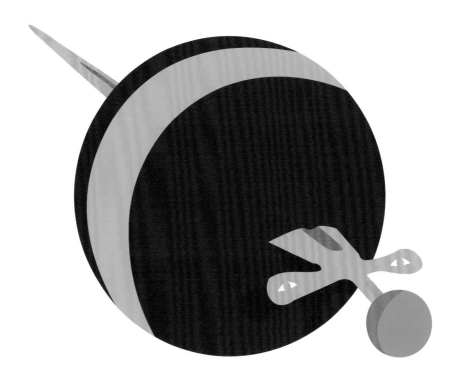

Is Angela's sepulcher scene an act of belief? Is it a ritual? Or a liturgy? Is it an ecstatic experience? A mystical experience? A transgression? Something else?

And is Angela's sepulcher scene scriptural? Is it scripted? Or is it improvised, unique?

Angela's performances—as performances of, or performances that are, "religion"— raise more questions than they answer. They pose more problems than solutions for studying religion. They trouble our term-tools. They make studying religion messy.

These are good things.

SPACE/

PLACE

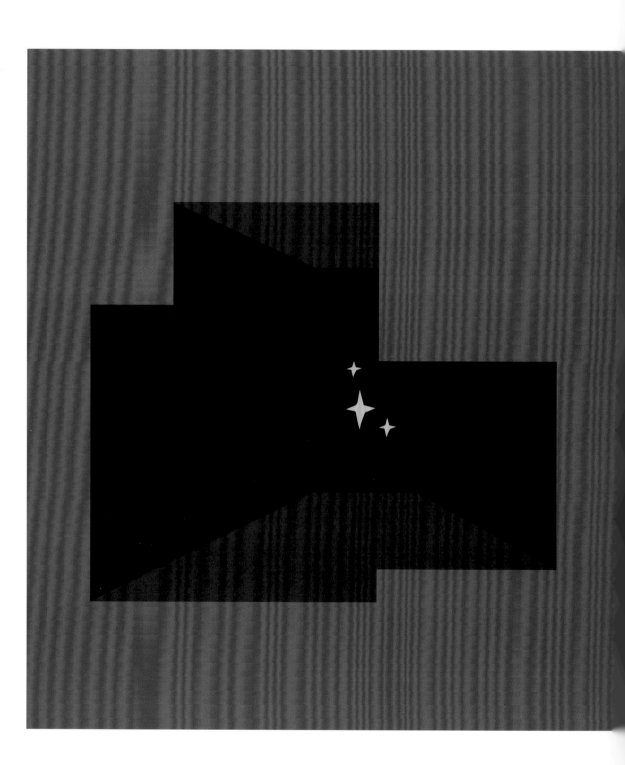

Space, to me, was freedom.

Imagining Sun Ra's world or listening to Earth, Wind and Fire transported me to another dimension. It probably did not help that I spent lots of time rereading *Chariots of the Gods* at an age far too young. I watched "In Search of. . ." with Leonard Nimoy hoping that someday those people who made the Nazca Lines or the Pyramids would come looking for me. I hoped that they would look just like me.

There was not a name for the way I felt at the time, but now there is: Afrofuturist.

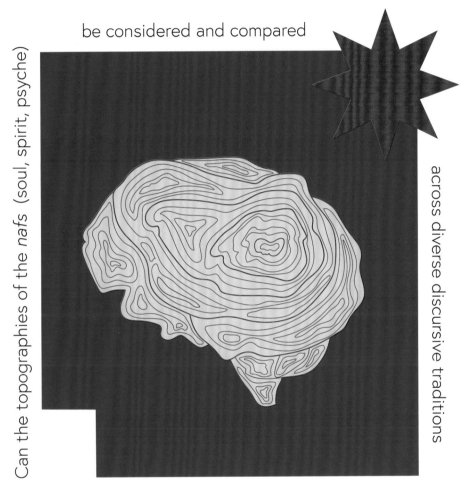

be considered and compared

Can the topographies of the *nafs* (soul, spirit, psyche)

across diverse discursive traditions

and intellectual formations?

If the *nafs* is, within this tradition, a space where the Divine can be manifested, then it is also a space for the potential transformation of the soul.

What is this space of transformation within Islamic practice and does it find echoes in the psychoanalytic space of the clinic?

[T]ranscendence literally means to climb above; *immanence*, by contrast, means "to dwell in" (from Latin *in* [in or into] and *manere* [to dwell]). So, the combination—immanent transcendence—suggests some perplexing idea of climbing above while dwelling within. But what could this possibly mean?

Most of the city's residents go about unaware

that they are enmeshed in
a vast web of surveillance

and move through
the urban landscape

on terms set

by the
conspiring
powerful.

✦ Meanwhile, the protagonists traverse the terrain laid out, on the shadow map, defying the constraints

of the imposed system of surveillance in an effort to defeat the system. ✦

Black people have produced
and navigated shadow maps
from the moment they were
forced onto North American
shores and into the expanding system of racial slavery.

They forged connections
with one another across
spaces of captivity by
creating pathways to avoid
white patrollers, and they
used the night sky as a guide
to map routes to free themselves from enslavement.

MODE

RNITY

Modernity is *our* era, for better or worse, and so stories of its emergence and descriptions of its character offer stories of ourselves.

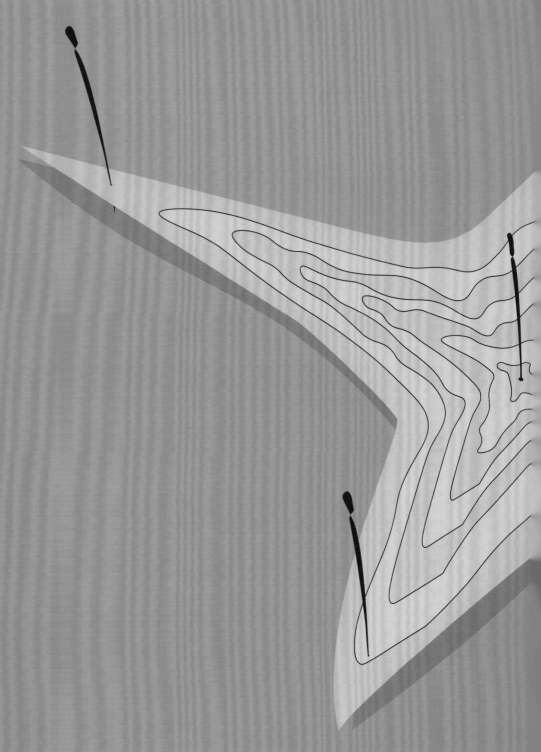

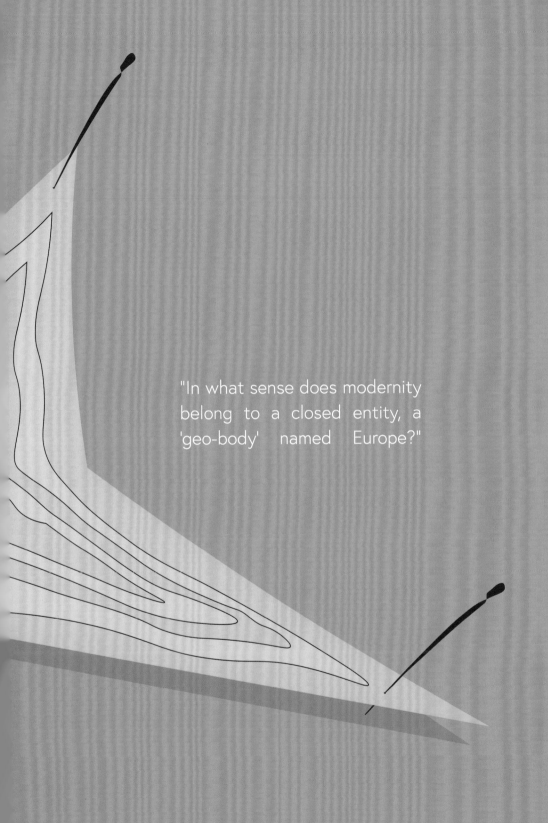

"In what sense does modernity belong to a closed entity, a 'geo-body' named Europe?"

"Naming a border is a way to rectify and absolve us,

it's a way to give credence to our own inaction

and to do so without shame.

A border can do the job of asserting the limits

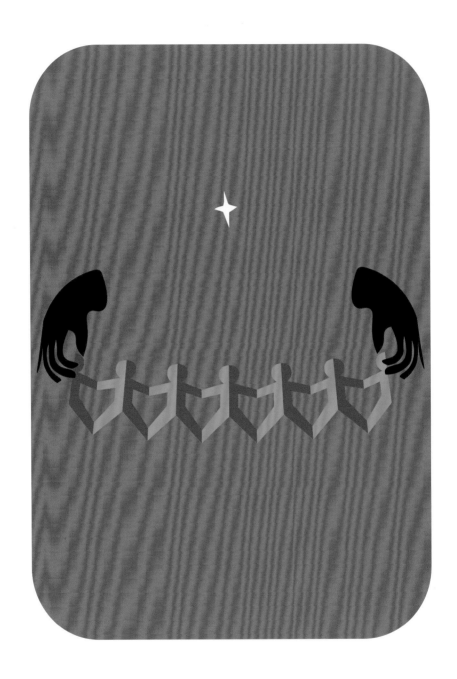

of our ethical obligation—where we are bound

and then miraculously, arbitrarily, not."

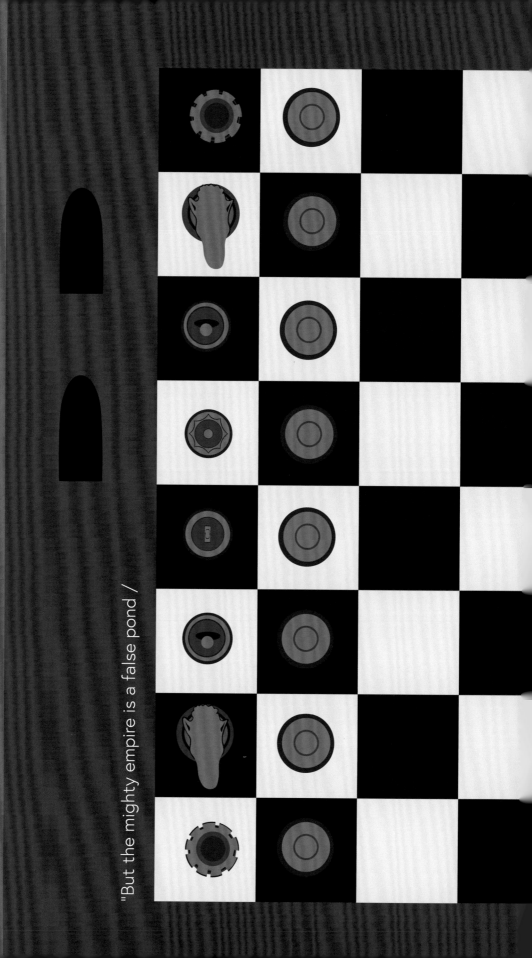

"But the mighty empire is a false pond /

in this eternal light where

night never descends, /

old travelers forever dying;

where we pass

their lamb-milk eyes / astonished

by years passing as one long noon."

"Beloved, she my daughter.
She mine. See. She come back
to me of her own free will and
I don't have to explain a thing."

ENCHAN
DISENCH

TMENT/
ANTMENT

Enchantment cannot exist without being conjured up by the project of disenchantment any more than the savage can exist without being conceived by civilization.

10:01

What's enchanting?

🌟🌟🌟🌟🌟🌟🌟🌟

14 characters over   Enchant

What's enchanting?

200 characters over   Enchant

A term is a fixed or finite period. And so, in the spirit of that particular meaning of "term," I invite us to consider whether maybe enchantment's current term is nearing an end. Our most brilliant writers and thinkers show us what we can do with it and what all its moves make possible to say. As we reach the end of this term, enchantment's claims to exhaustiveness become exhausting.

10:04

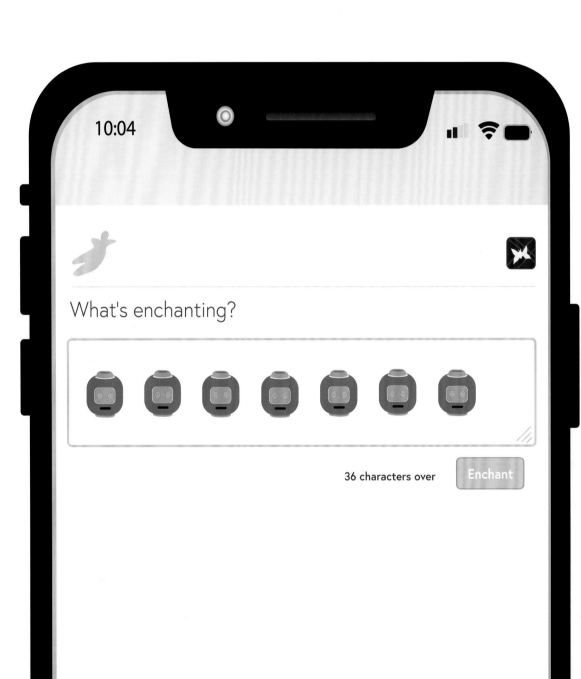

What's enchanting?

36 characters over   Enchant

So, are there other ways to consider the stuff that has been marked as modernity's surpluses? Are there other terms (with their own term limits) that enable us to think this stuff otherwise—that is, without invoking the readymade distinctions contained in "enchantment"?

Abjection
Abomination
Acme
Allure
Ambient
Amnesis
Anamnesis
Animal spirits
Apophasia
Apophenia
Arousal
Attraction
Augury
Binge
Boredom
Captive
Carnival
Charisma
Compotation
Compulsion
Conjure
Contempt
Cyborg
Demonic
Diabolism
Disgust
Doppelgänger

Dream
Drunk
Ecstasy
Engorgement
Enthrallment
Euphoria
Excess
Excrement
Expenditure
Fling
Fluid
Future
Gargantuan
G
r
a
v
i
t
a
t
i
o
n
Hallucination
Hex
Horror
Humors
Inattention
Invocation

Jinx
Kink
Leftover
Legerdemain
Love
Lure
Magic
Magnetism

Malediction
Melancholy
Monster
Nimiety
Obeah
Otherwise
Parasite
Passion
Phantasm
Phlegm
Possess
Presence
Prestidigitation
Prophecy
Queer
Rapture
Ravish
Risk
Rupture

Seduction
Shadow
Sortilege
Spectral
Spell
Sprinkles
Superfluous
Surplus
Swamp
Sybaritic
Tangent
Terror
Thaumaturgy
Uncanny
Utopia
Vestige
Visceral
Viscous
Votive
Wake
Witch
Whammy
Wound
X
Yes
Yeti

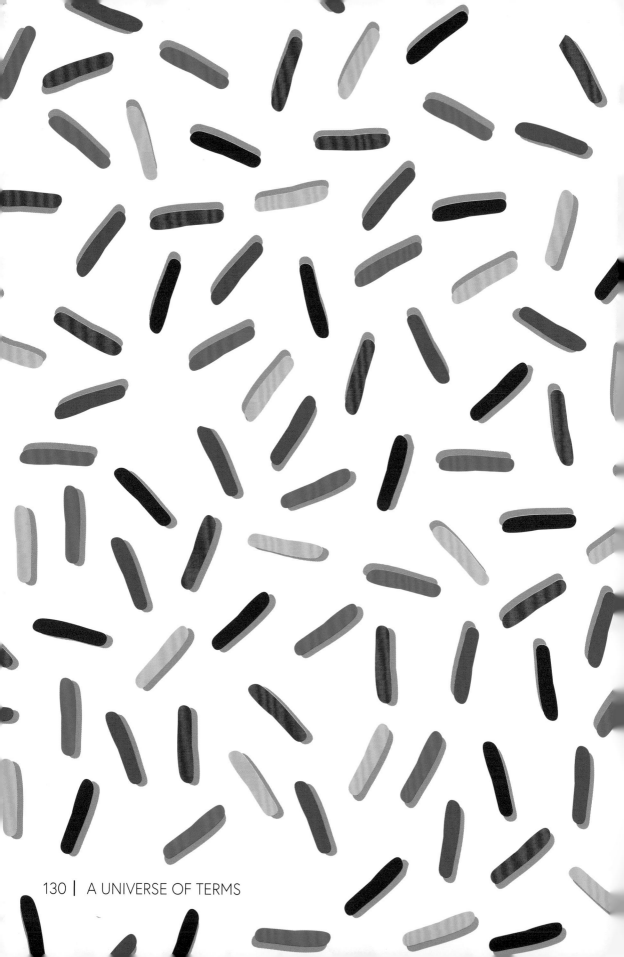

B A

M A T

Index

SPIRIT

Emily Ogden [5-8] : Whatever *spirit* is—and the term has many meanings—you usually have to get rid of some other encumbering things in order to get at it. . . . The spirit of Spirit, if you will, is demolition. . . . The castle in the air is theirs to kick. The moth skates through the damaged web. Demolition actually works this time.

Ogden, Emily. "spirit." *The Immanent Frame*. November 14, 2019. https://tif. ssrc .org/2019/11/14/spirit-ogden/

Paul Christopher Johnson [9-13] : The Spiritual Exercises. The Spirit of 1776. Spirit of an age, *Zeitgeist*. We've got spirit! A spirited opposition. Spiritual awakening. Spiritual warfare. The Spirit of Christmas Past. *Esprit de corps*. Spirit possession. Spirit Airlines. Holy Spirit. Espírito Santo, Brazil. 'Whoa, spirit / Watch the heavens open (yeah) / Spirit, can you hear it callin'?' sings Beyoncé. Karl Marx: We are infused by the spirit of the state. Émile Durkheim's spirit of society. Conception among the Arunta, wrote Sigmund Freud, is experienced as a reincarnated spirit entering the mother's body. Spiritism. Smells like teen spirit. Spirit-writing. Spirited away. Such a free spirit. . . . That's the spirit! Ancestor spirit. And the Spirit of God moved upon the face of the waters. 'Shop Esprit for dresses, tops, pants, skirts, shoes and accessories.' Spirit gives a name to outside forces that impinge on inner will. Even more, it undoes the very idea of a discrete split between inner and outer. . . . Like wind or breath, spirits make ionic bonds, grabbing electrons from each other's circuits to form new semantic clouds. . . .

[S]pirit is never only gaseous or metaphysical. It always links up with *things*, like airline, writing, teen, face of the waters, pants. Then, too, spirit moves in verbs like incorporate, possess, descend, hover, fill, and have. And spirit settles near adjectives like holy, ancestral, or free. Verbs and adjectives materialize and spatialize an otherwise vaporous word. They turn spirit tangible, push it into text and flesh incarnate.

Johnson, Paul Christopher. "spirit." *The Immanent Frame*. November 14, 2019. https://tif.ssrc.org/2019/11/14/spirit-johnson/

Josef Sorett [14-17] : What happens when spirit(s) is tethered to an adjective? A racial modifier, for instance? Does making spirit black help to clarify things? . . . [T]he spirit of religion in America is, as one historian put it, "the encounter of black and white."

Sorett, Josef. "spirit." *The Immanent Frame*. November 14, 2019. https://tif .ssrc.org/2019/11/14/spirit-sorett/

ECONOMY

Kathryn Lofton [21-23] : Economy is not about money or things. Economy is the practice of constraint toward money and toward things. Economy is a synonym for denial, for constraint, for restraint. . . . Particular religions feel differently about payroll. But every religion counsels on how not to be controlled by coin.

Lofton, Kathryn. "economy." *The Immanent Frame*. January 17, 2020. https:// tif.ssrc.org/2020/01/17/economy-lofton/

Amira Mittermaier [24-29] : Writing about the commodity, Marx used adjectives such as queer, metaphysical, theological, transcendent, mystical, fantastic, and magical (or, in the German original, *vertrackt, metaphysisch, theologisch, mysteriös, übersinnlich, wunderlich, mystisch, rätselhaft, geheimnisvoll*). . . . What might it mean to think of the economy with the gods and spirits fully present? How can we take seriously the queer, mystical, metaphysical, and theological underpinnings (and iterations) of the economy? . . . *Not secularizing* the economy means leaving space for the gods and spirits whenever and wherever they turn up. . . . Here, divine action (and not a fetishized "economy") decenters human labor.

Mittermaier, Amira. "economy." *The Immanent Frame.* January 17, 2020. https://tif.ssrc.org/2020/01/17/economy-mittermaier/

Webb Keane [30-33] : The scriptural assertion that "the poor you will always have with you" leads back from the God's eye perspective to the second person of address, "you," and its partner, the first person plural, "us." And these pronouns bring us back to the street, where the most visible of the poor challenge the passerby to ask: Do you count as one of us?

Keane, Webb. "economy." *The Immanent Frame.* January 17, 2020. https://tif.ssrc.org/2020/01/17/economy-keane/

HUMAN

Christine Helmer [37-39] : Human living—resistance in the face of the inevitable, and orientation to love in the face of annihilation. Theologians look to those places of resilience. They wonder at glimpses of dignity amid the decrepitude. Human living is a daily struggle to make ends meet; a blank stare into an unlit tunnel; the horror at what is unspeakable yet real.

Helmer, Christine. "human." *The Immanent Frame.* March 13, 2020. https://tif.ssrc.org/2020/06/26/human-helmer/

Winnifred Fallers Sullivan [40-41] : What are crosses? Can crosses—can *the* cross—be a sign of the human? . . . The cross came to be understood as preceding and prefiguring the Christ. In other words, those who study the cross see a deeply ambiguous and shifting symbol, one not easily reduced to either religious or secular.

Sullivan, Winnifred Fallers. "human." *The Immanent Frame*. March 13, 2020. https://tif.ssrc.org/2020/03/13/human-sullivan/

Constance Furey [42-44] : In her essential article about how humanity came to be a racist category, Sylvia Wynter identifies Luther's era as a turning point. When Renaissance humanists "degodded" man, Wynter argues, the human became a biocentric category. Absent God, she observes, "Race becomes the answer that the secularizing West would now give to the Heideggerian question as to the who, and the what we are." . . . I do not think, as Wynter implies, that having a god keeps humans in check, but instead that putting a god or gods in the mix might help us to think the human better.

Furey, Constance. "human." *The Immanent Frame*. March 13, 2020. https://tif.ssrc.org/2020/03/13/human-furey/

Abou Farman [45-47] : [H]uman forces driving catastrophic climate change—an era known as the Anthropocene—makes the human doubt the future it had claimed as its domain to shape, the control and mastery it once thought it would exercise over the architecture of the future, the freedom it promised itself in opening up the future beyond destiny and fate. . . . [T]here is no universal human world that is going to end; rather, under the rhetoric of universal humanity, people are mobilizing, again, to save particular worlds from destruction. . . . Which human world do you want to see end?

Farman, Abou. "human." *The Immanent Frame*. March 13, 2020. https://tif.ssrc.org/2020/03/13/human-farman/

MEDIA

John Durham Peters [51-55] : In 1963, my parents, with three kids (aged five, three, and one) in tow and one more on the way. . . got a small black-

and-white television set. . . . TV signals would bounce off of buildings, creating small lags in transmission and *Doppelgänger* on screen, but often the signals would never even arrive, leaving us with no more picture than an apocalyptic scene of warring ants jousting at high-speed. . . . Media vary historically. . . . Nothing's quite as spooky as logging into Wi-Fi in a hotel or apartment building and seeing all those anonymously intimate networks pop up, a broadcast Kabbalah of secret names and private jokes you will never be privy to. . . . Media turn on borders and interfaces. . . . Media have grammars. . . . Media combine nature and culture. . . . Media have ontological effects.

Peters, John Durham. "media." *The Immanent Frame*. February 14, 2020. http://tif.ssrc.org/2020/02/14/media-peters/

Nathan Schneider [56-57] : Just when you thought you had your phone in a box, its logic fills your brainstorms. Just when religion seemed defined and dispensed with, a new kind of salvation beckons.

Schneider, Nathan. "media." *The Immanent Frame*. February 14, 2020. http://tif.ssrc.org/2020/02/14/media-schneider/

Birgit Meyer [58-65] : What might happen when we put the discarded *legbawo* of the Ewe, and similar images of other African peoples, in conversation with the discarded images of Mary and Jesus (as done by way of experiment in the Bode Museum Berlin)? What might these objects, that became "matter out of place" in their present, secular contexts, tell us about human striving for power and powers in our deeply entangled, postcolonial world? How do such old religious media matter in secular contexts? Which memories, stories, and powers can they mediate and transmit?

Meyer, Birgit. "media." *The Immanent Frame*. February 14, 2020. http://tif .ssrc.org/2020/02/14/media-meyer/

PERFORMANCE

Paul Yachnin [69-75] : A performance is some kind of action that changes something in the real world. . . ."Performance" also means play-acting, doing or saying something that changes nothing in the real world . . . . [W]e could say that Shakespeare's theatrical faith workshop became a space for "communicative action." . . . Shakespeare's faith workshop . . . invited the playgoers to give expression to their religious feeling and thinking by way of their responses to the action unfolding on stage, to recognize the different faith-based emotions and thoughts of other playgoers, and to begin to grasp how faith itself is performed—both accomplished as a real thing in the world and play-acted as an invention of the mind.

Yachnin, Paul. "performance." *The Immanent Frame*. December 20, 2019. https://tif.ssrc.org/2019/12/20/performance-yachnin/

Vaughn A. Booker [76-77] : A musical call and response between brass and reeds opens the 1933 composition for Cab Calloway and His Orchestra, "Harlem Camp Meeting." A voice asks, "What's this comin' off here?" and after a brief pause, reflects, "It's more like one of them good ol' revival days here. A camp meeting! Yowza, yowza!" Next comes a clarinet solo, and the inquiring voice assumes the role of a narrator in remarking, "There's a dear brother got happy on that clarinet, look at him. Greeeat day!" As the clarinet solo continues, the narrator interjects affirmative responses: "Tell me all about it, brother. Tell me all about it, now." The narrator then refers to the "brother" as "son" and tells him to "Get ready for this scat sermon I'm gonna give you here." The narrator produces a wordless vocal melody, accompanied by syncopated chimes replicating the sound of distant Sunday church bells.

Booker, Vaughn A. "performance." *The Immanent Frame*. December 20, 2019. https://tif.ssrc.org/author/vaughn-a-booker/

William Robert [78-83] : On Holy Saturday 1294, an Umbrian woman found herself in a sepulcher with Christ's dead body. The woman kissed Christ's breast, then Christ's mouth. She placed her cheek on Christ's cheek. Then Christ placed his hand on her other cheek. Christ pressed the woman's body close to his in an embrace. Christ whispered lovingly to the woman, though Christ's eyes and lips remained closed. The woman was Angela of Foligno (c. 1248–1309), a widow, a lay Franciscan, a mystic. Angela's sepulcher scene came in the twenty-fourth step of her twenty-six-step spiritual itinerary. Her itinerary included other extraordinary scenes. Angela denuded herself before a crucifix. She saw eyes appear in eucharistic bread-bodies. She bathed lepers, then drank the bathing water. She drank blood from, and later entered, Christ's side wound. . . . Is Angela's sepulcher scene an act of belief? Is it a ritual? Or a liturgy? Is it an ecstatic experience? A mystical experience? A transgression? Something else? And is Angela's sepulcher scene scriptural? Is it scripted? Or is it improvised, unique? . . . Angela's performances—as performances of, or performances that are, "religion"—raise more questions than they answer. They pose more problems than solutions for studying religion. They trouble our term-tools. They make studying religion messy. These are good things.

Robert, William. "performance." *The Immanent Frame*. December 20, 2019. https://tif.ssrc.org/2019/12/20/performance-robert/

SPACE/PLACE

Anthea Butler [87-88] : Space, to me, was freedom. Imagining Sun Ra's world or listening to Earth, Wind and Fire transported me to another dimension. It probably did not help that I spent lots of time rereading *Chariots of the Gods* at an age far too young. I watched "In Search of . . ." with Leonard Nimoy hoping that someday those people who made the Nazca Lines or the Pyramids would come looking for me. I hoped that they would look just like me. . . . There was not a name for the way I felt at the time, but now there is: Afrofuturist.

Butler, Anthea. "Space is all there is." *The Immanent Frame*. March 6, 2018. http://tif.ssrc.org/2018/03/06/space-is-all-there-is/

Omnia El Shakry [89-91] : Can the topographies of the *nafs* (soul, spirit, psyche) be considered and compared across diverse discursive traditions and intellectual formations? . . . If the *nafs* is, within this tradition, a space where the Divine can be manifested, then it is also a space for the potential transformation of the soul. What is this space of transformation within Islamic practice and does it find echoes in the psychoanalytic space of the clinic?

El Shakry, Omnia. "A liturgy of the soul." *The Immanent Frame*. November 1, 2018. http://tif.ssrc.org/2018/11/01/a-liturgy-of-the-soul/

Mark Cauchi [92-93] : [T]ranscendence literally means to climb above; *immanence*, by contrast, means "to dwell in" (from Latin *in* [in or into] and *manere* [to dwell]). So, the combination—immanent transcendence—suggests some perplexing idea of climbing above while dwelling within. But what could this possibly mean?

Cauchi, Mark. "What's more? or, An answer to the question 'Is this all there is?'" *The Immanent Frame*. November 20, 2017. https://tif.ssrc.org/2017/11/20/whats-more/

Judith Weisenfeld [94-97] : Most of the city's residents go about unaware that they are enmeshed in a vast web of surveillance and move through the urban landscape on terms set by the conspiring powerful. Meanwhile, the protagonists traverse the terrain laid out on the shadow map, defying the constraints of the imposed system of surveillance in an effort to defeat the system. . . . Black people have produced and navigated shadow maps from the moment they were forced onto North American shores and into the expanding system of racial slavery. They forged connections with one another across spaces of captivity by creating pathways to avoid white patrollers, and they used the night sky as a guide to map routes to free themselves from enslavement.

Weisenfeld, Judith. "space, place." *The Immanent Frame*. February 28, 2019. https://tif.ssrc.org/2020/02/28/space-place-weisenfeld/

MODERNITY

Jonathan Sheehan [101] : Modernity is *our* era, for better or worse, and so stories of its emergence and descriptions of its character offer stories of ourselves.

Sheehan, Jonathan. "modernity." *The Immanent Frame*. June 12, 2020. https://tif.ssrc.org/2020/06/12/modernity-sheehan/

Nancy Levene [102-115] : "In what sense does modernity belong to a closed entity, a 'geo-body' named Europe?" . . . "Naming a border is a way to rectify and absolve us, it's a way to give credence to our own inaction and to do so without shame. A border can do the job of asserting the limits of our ethical obligation—where we are bound and then miraculously, arbitrarily, not." . . . "Beloved, she my daughter. She mine. See. She come back to me of her own free will and I don't have to explain a thing." . . . "But the mighty empire is a false pond / in this eternal light where night never descends, / where we pass old travelers forever dying, their lamb-milk eyes / astonished by years passing as one long noon."

Levene, Nancy. "modernity." *The Immanent Frame*. June 12, 2020. https://tif.ssrc.org/2020/06/12/modernity-levene/

ENCHANTMENT/DISENCHANTMENT

Susan Lepselter [119-121] : Enchantment cannot exist without being conjured up by the project of disenchantment any more than the savage can exist without being conceived by civilization.

Lepselter, Susan. "Pay no mind to that man behind the curtain!" *The Immanent Frame*. March 29, 2019. https://tif.ssrc.org/2019/03/29/pay-no-atten tion-to-that-man-behind-the-curtain/

Courtney Bender [122-131] : A term is a fixed or finite period. And so, in the spirit of that particular meaning of "term," I invite us to consider whether maybe enchantment's current term is nearing an end. Our most brilliant writers and thinkers show us what we can do with it and what all its moves make possible to say. As we reach the end of this term, enchantment's claims to exhaustiveness become exhausting. . . . So, are there other ways to consider the stuff that has been marked as modernity's surpluses? Are there other terms (with their own term limits) that enable us to think this stuff otherwise—that is, without invoking the readymade distinctions contained in "enchantment"? . . . Abjection Abomination Acme Allure Ambient Amnesis Anamnesis Animal spirits Apophasia Apophenia Arousal Attraction Augury Binge Boredom Captive Carnival Charisma Compotation Compulsion Conjure Contempt Cyborg Demonic Diabolism Disgust Döppelganger Dream Drunk Ecstasy Engorgement Enthrallment Euphoria Excess Excrement Expenditure Fling Fluid Future Gargantuan Gravitation Hallucination Hex Horror Humors Inattention Invocation Jinx Kink Leftover Legerdemain Love Lure Magic Magnetism Malediction Melancholy Monster Nimiety Obeah Otherwise Parasite Passion Phantasm Phlegm Possess Presence Prestidigitation Prophecy Queer Rapture Ravish Risk Rupture Seduction Shadow Sortilege Spectral Spell Sprinkles Superfluous Surplus Swamp Sybaritic Tangent Terror Thaumaturgy Uncanny Utopia Vestige   Visceral Viscous Votive Wake Witch Whammy Wound X Yes Yeti

Bender, Courtney. "enchantment/disenchantment." *The Immanent Frame*. May 1, 2020. https://tif.ssrc.org/2020/05/01/enchantment-disenchantment-bender/

Bibliography

GRAPHIC NONFICTION

Abirached, Zeina. *A Game for Swallows: To Die, To Leave, To Return.* Translated by Edward Gauvin. Minneapolis: Graphic Universe, 2012.

———. *I Remember Beirut.* Translated by Edward Gauvin. Minneapolis: Graphic Universe, 2014.

Abirached, Zeina, and Mathias Enard. *Prendre refuge.* Paris: CASTERMAN, 2018.

Doxiadis, Apostolos, and Christos H. Papadimitrou. *Logicomix: An Epic Search for Truth.* New York: Bloomsbury, 2009.

Filiu, Jean-Pierre, and David B. *The Best of Enemies: A History of US and Middle East Relations.* 3 vols. London: SelfMadeHero, 2012–2018.

Findakly, Brigitte, and Lewis Trondheim. *Poppies of Iraq.* Translated by Helge Dascher. Montreal: Drawn and Quarterly, 2017.

Hamdy, Sherine, and Coleman Nye. *Lissa: A Story about Medical Promise, Friendship, and Revolution.* Toronto: University of Toronto Press, 2017.

Lomasko, Victoria. *Other Russias.* New York: n+1 Foundation, 2017.

Sattouf, Riad. *Arab of the Future.* 4 vols. Translated by Sam Taylor. New York: Metropolitan Books, 2015–2020.

Satrapi, Marjane. *Persepolis*. New York: Pantheon Books, 2003.

Sousanis, Nick. *Unflattening*. Cambridge, MA: Harvard University Press, 2015.

Strunk Jr., William E., and E. B. White. *The Elements of Style*. Illustrated by Maira Kalman. New York: Penguin Press, 2007.

Ziadé, Lamia. *Bye Bye Babylon: Beirut 1975–1979*. Northampton, MA: Interlink Publishing Group, 2012.

GRAPHIC FICTION

Shakespeare, William. *Hamlet*. Illustrated by Aki Kuroda. Translated by Jean-Michel Dé-prats. Paris: GALLIMARD, 2016.

EXHIBITIONS, SELECTED ARTWORKS, AND CATALOGS

Bolton, Andrew, and Michael Chabon. *Superheroes: Fashion and Fantasy*. New York : New Haven: Metropolitan Museum of Art, 2008.

Bolton, Andrew, Sølve Sundsbø, Tim Blanks, and Susannah Frankel. *Alexander McQueen: Savage Beauty*. New York and New Haven: Metropolitan Museum of Art/Yale University Press, 2011.

Calder, Alexander, *Calder's Circus, 1926–1931*, Wire, wood, metal, cloth, yarn, paper, cardboard, leather, string, rubber tubing, corks, buttons, rhinestones, pipe cleaners, and bottle caps, The Whitney Museum, New York City, accessed November 26, 2008.

Godfrey, Mark. *Alighiero e Boetti*. New Haven and London: Yale University Press, 2011.

Godfrey, Mark, and Zoé Whitley. *Soul of a Nation: Art in the Age of Black Power*. New York: D.A.P Publishing/TATE, 2017.

Jallon, Benoît, Umberto Napolitano, and Franck Boutté, eds. *Paris Haussman: modèle de ville*. Paris/Zürich: Pavillon de l'Arsenal/Park Books, 2017.

LAN Local Architecture Network, Benoît Jallon, Umberto Napolitano, and Le Laboratoire R. A. A. R., eds. *Napoli Super Modern*. Zürich: Park Books, 2020.

Matisse, Henri. *Jazz*. Paris: Editions de la Martinière, 2013.

Molesworth, Helen, Ian Alteveer, Abigail Winograd, and Dieter Roesltraete. *Kerry James Marshall: Mastry*. New York: Skira Rizzoli, 2016.

Mutu, Wangechi. *A Promise to Communicate*. Madrid: Ivorypress, 2019.

Sher, Max, Kate Bush, Max Trudolubov, and Nuria Fatykhova, eds. *Palimpsest*. Moscow: Ad Marginem, 2018.

Tsai, Eugene, ed. *Kehinde Wiley: A New Republic*. Munich and New York: Prestel/Brooklyn Museum, 2015.

LITERATURE

Al Rawi, Shahad. *The Baghdad Clock*. Translated by Luke Leafgren. Hardback Edition. London: Oneworld Publications, 2018.

Lalami, Laila. *The Other Americans*. New York: Pantheon Books, 2019.

Morrison, Toni. *Beloved*. New York: Alfred A. Knopf, 1987.

Powers, Richard. *The Overstory*. New York: W. W. Norton & Company, 2018.

Ward, Jesmyn. *Salvage the Bones*. New York: Bloomsbury, 2011.

LITERARY COLLECTIONS

Cole, Teju. *Blind Spot*. New York: Penguin Random House, 2017.

Gornick, Vivian. *Approaching Eye Level*. New York: Picador, 1996.

Hamid, Mohsin. *Discontent and Its Civilizations: Dispatches from Lahore, New York, and London*. New York: Riverhead Books, 2015.

Hong, Cathy Park. *Minor Feelings: An Asian American Reckoning*. New York: Open World, 2020.

Rankine, Claudia. *Citizen: An American Lyric*. Minneapolis: Graywolf Press, 2014.

——— . *Just Us: An American Conversation*. Minneapolis: Graywolf Press, 2020.

PODCASTS

Abdelfatah, Rund, and Ramteen Arablouei, hosts. "The Mask," *Throughline* (podcast). May 14, 2020. Accessed May 14, 2020. https://www.npr .org/2020/05/13/855405132/the-mask

Mars, Roman, host. "Goodnight Nobody," *99% Invisible* (podcast). September 29, 2020. Accessed September 29, 2020. https://99percentinvisible .org/episode/goodnight-nobody/

Mputubwele, Ngofeen and Gregory Warner, hosts. "We Don't Say That," *Rough Translation* (podcast). May 1, 2019. Accessed February 10, 2020. https://www.npr.org/2019/04/30/718729150/we-dont-say-that

Newkirk II, Van R., host. "Part III: Through the Looking Glass," *Floodlines* (podcast). March 3-12, 2020. Accessed May 30, 2020. https://www.theat lantic.com/podcasts/floodlines/

Zaltzman, Helen, host. "Engraving Part 1: Epitaph," *The Allusionist* (podcast). November 26, 2019. Accessed June 26, 2020. https://www.theallu sionist .org/allusionist/epitaph

ABOUT THE AUTHORS

Mona Oraby is Assistant Professor of Political Science at Howard University and Editor of *The Immanent Frame*, a digital publication of the Social Science Research Council that advances scholarly debate on secularism, religion, and the public sphere.

Emilie Flamme is a graduate of Amherst College, where she double-majored in Architectural Studies and Russian. She is a researcher and illustrator based in the United States and France.

ABOUT THE TYPE

This book was set in Europa, a sans serif typeface created in 2011 by Fabian Leuenberger. Europa combines two popular European typefaces: Futura and Gill Sans.